GOODS AND SERVICES

by Marne Ventura

Cody Koala

An Imprint of Pop!
popbooksonline.com

abdopublishing.com

Published by Pop!, a division of ABDO, PO Box 398166, Minneapolis, Minnesota 55439. Copyright © 2019 by POP, LLC. International copyrights reserved in all countries. No part of this book may be reproduced in any form without written permission from the publisher. Pop!™ is a trademark and logo of POP, LLC.

Printed in the United States of America, North Mankato, Minnesota

032018
092018

THIS BOOK CONTAINS RECYCLED MATERIALS

Cover Photo: iStockphoto
Interior Photos: Shutterstock Images, 5, 7 (top), 7 (bottom left), 7 (bottom right), 8, 13, 14, 17, 18, 20 (left), 20 (right), 21 (right); Chris Dillmann/Vail Daily via AP, 11; iStockphoto, 21 (left)

Editor: Charly Haley
Series Designer: Laura Mitchell

Library of Congress Control Number: 2017963364

Publisher's Cataloging-in-Publication Data

Names: Ventura, Marne, author.
Title: Goods and services / by Marne Ventura.
Description: Minneapolis, Minnesota : Pop!, 2019. | Series: Community economics |
Includes online resources and index.
Identifiers: ISBN 9781532160028 (lib.bdg.) | ISBN 9781532161148 (ebook) |
Subjects: LCSH: Consumer goods--Juvenile literature. | Community development--Juvenile literature. | Regional economics--Juvenile literature. | Economic development--Juvenile literature. | Community life--Juvenile literature.
Classification: DDC 330.9--dc23

Hello! My name is
Cody Koala

Pop open this book and you'll find QR codes like this one, loaded with information, so you can learn even more!

Scan this code* and others like it while you read, or visit the website below to make this book pop.

popbooksonline.com/goods-and-services

*Scanning QR codes requires a web-enabled smart device with a QR code reader app and a camera.

Table of Contents

Goods

Goods are things that people buy with money. Hannah buys eggs for breakfast. Brandon buys a book to read. Those are examples of goods.

Watch a video here!

Making Goods

Many goods are made in factories. Then they go to stores for people to buy them.

Learn more here!

Maria buys a toy at a store. The toy was made in a factory.

Sometimes goods are sold by the people who make them. An artist makes a painting. She sells it to someone by herself. The painting doesn't have to go to a store first.

Chapter 3

Services

A server brings dinner to people at a restaurant. A mechanic fixes someone's car. A doctor checks someone's health.

Complete an activity here!

Servers, mechanics, and doctors all provide services. They work to do things for other people. They are paid money for their work.

The way all people act together to make, buy, and sell goods and services is called the **economy**.

Chapter 4

Providing Services

Sometimes people pay directly for a service. Lynn pays her piano teacher for lessons.

A person buying goods or services is called a **consumer**.

Learn more here!

Sometimes people pay indirectly for a service. Marcus goes to a bakery to buy bread, which is a good. But Marcus is also paying the baker for the service of baking the bread.

1

A toy is a good. It was made in a factory.

2

The toy is sent to a store for people to buy it.

When people buy goods at a store, the store gets money. The store uses some of the money to pay its **cashiers**.

A cashier helps Emma's mom buy the toy. The cashier provides a service.

Emma gets to bring the toy home.

The cashiers provide a service to people shopping at the store.

Making Connections

Text-to-Self

What are some goods and services that your family buys?

Text-to-Text

Have you read a book in which a character bought something? Was it a good or a service?

Text-to-World

How have you seen people making goods or providing services in the real world?

Glossary

cashier – a person who collects money when people buy things at a store.

consumer – a person who buys goods or services.

economy – the way all people act together to make, buy, and sell goods and services.

goods – things that people use money to buy.

services – actions provided to other people that workers are paid to do.

Index

consumer, 16

economy, 15

factories, 6, 9, 20

goods, 4, 6, 10, 15, 16, 19–20

money, 4, 15, 20

services, 12, 15, 16, 19, 21

stores, 6, 9, 10, 20–21

work, 15

Online Resources

popbooksonline.com

Thanks for reading this Cody Koala book!

Scan this code* and others like it in this book, or visit the website below to make this book pop!

popbooksonline.com/goods-and-services

*Scanning QR codes requires a web-enabled smart device with a QR code reader app and a camera.